DAY

GLO

WINNER OF THE SAWTOOTH POETRY PRIZE

2010

TERRANCE HAYES, JUDGE

DAYGLO

JAMES MEETZE

AHSAHTA PRESS

BOISE, IDAHO 2011

Ahsahta Press, Boise State University
Boise, Idaho 83725-1525
http://ahsahtapress.boisestate.edu
http://ahsahtapress.boisestate.edu/books/meetze/meetze.htm

Printed in the United States of America
Cover design by Quemadura
Cover photography by Jack Pierson
Book design by Janet Holmes
First printing January 2011
ISBN-13: 978-1-934103-18-0

Library of Congress Cataloging-in-Publication Data

Meetze, James, 1977-
 Dayglo / James Meetze.
   p. cm.
 "Winner of the Sawtooth Poetry Prize 2010."
 ISBN-13: 978-1-934103-18-0 (pbk. : alk. paper)
 ISBN-10: 1-934103-18-7 (pbk. : alk. paper)
 I. Title.
 PS3613.E376D39 2011
 811'.6--DC22
                            2010032771

ACKNOWLEDGMENTS

Some of these poems have previously appeared, often in earlier drafts, in the following publications: *A Public Space, Modern Review, Sand Canyon Review, Sprung Formal, The Latent Print, Tight, Tinfoil Dresses,* and *Vertebrae.* "It's Overhead" appeared as a limited-edition chapbook from Fashionably Pressed (2007).

*There is no place for the man whose steps head
toward his place of birth*

—Edmond Jabès

Cities summarize us

—Robin Blaser

CONTENTS

GREEN

NEGATIVE THINKING

DAYGLO

FINEST CITY

NOTES

ABOUT THE AUTHOR

GREEN

IT'S OVERHEAD

Looking up at it

all that energy

tumbling upon you

makes you pucker up

and hope the light

those green rays

of light are waiting

at the exit.

Its cool rapture

like having a job

you'd kill for

but you have it

(tenuously).

Where weird stars

poke fun at your mica eyes.

That bright star alone

in the sky.

Warming everything

the sand, the esplanade

the green light, the asphalt

warming even you.

+

A windfall of water
can be remembered
as just a wave.
But to look into memory
things begin to sparkle
like so many pair of eyes
looking at you
as a compass in the night.
Looking toward whichever
magnetic pole you lean
in the dancing fog-light.
Poetry too is subject
to fogginess and wobble.
Our beacons never near
enough to illuminate
what we don't know.
We remember what it is
to be bathed in light,
to read and be changed.
The book is not an iceberg,
but the sound of breaking things.

+

A wave isn't only a gesture

but a signal that earth, too

pulsates and breathes.

Hello seafoam, hello

sandpiper, beachy stuff.

See the filtered light,

how it bends just enough

to fool the mind.

The color of sand

the color of a thought

in each deconstructed shell

a wave's synetic mate.

Glass-bottom green

seagrass loops and sound

of a breathing world.

To train the swimmer's ear

to recognize harmonic

reason travels faster

beneath water, a book of water

wet with ideas of summer.

A watery leisure time, now.

+

Looking up, then sunspots

trace everything you see

from green neon skyline

to a renovation project

in the burned down tire shop.

Every old corner,

a ghostlamp and lonely

big windows.

The light they let in.

How it behaves on dust.

Sunlit dustlight grey.

Lines of sun on the plaza.

Looking up at the words.

The sun's effect

on the body

then naptime during lecture.

The effect of working

or fuzzy halos in your eyes

give the sky serifs

where anything then.

Anything now.

+

To speak underwater or

to echolocate a companion

you become the conductor of a sound

only ever dreamt of.

To speak of ideas more grand

than a man-made island or

to fold leaves into a vessel

and carry water in it.

The cellulose Grecian green

like an urn you know.

Laurel green crown

on your nude subject

on the lawn.

Any subject is or isn't matter

is the idea of matter

the unattainable mist, the ether.

Wanting to garden indoors with you

and your photographic memory.

Looking up to hear the foghorn and breathe.

Someone is approaching

in the mist, someone is making a pose.

+

To bend you like light
in water, green boughs
bend too.
Afloat in flowers
in a heap of color
and greenery.
To be taken by a wave
so cinematically washed over
its aperture closing around you.
To desire to bend so
to be green, to be new
buds opening, light pouring in.
To fill memory's frame
or to bend you lengthwise
looking up at it
a clear and infinite ceiling.
To think this a big no-no
but clouds love
what they enshadow
like a train, just
seconds behind a white gown.

+

You reach for the crash
the water, the sun, the green
all combined in a day.
Bright and gray, Tuesday.
It contains every possible
combination of things:
pine needle, home, love.
It's the job
you'd do anything for.
It's always above
and looking down
at the small moving circles.
How you reach for them
with a wave between you.
Every afternoon sun's heat
carries a little breeze
it turns the pages
and takes the words elsewhere.
There is music in every hollow
in the space you fill
and in what you love now.

NEGATIVE THINKING

I showed you my field

I said this is my field

But you weren't impressed

—Mojave 3

TO SHARE THIS WEIRD SUN

In our city of a yard, or whatever

lark we might be onto

we always say (inescapably)

we're almost there,

but it's only weather, only gold.

Like how the sciences are

offing the humanities.

In this old building with

these new buildings around us.

I think there's too much

gold in everyone's eyes

when they drive,

like too much sun in the air.

Every neighborhood a freeway away.

So at home, the lawn is like

this giant forest below us

we waste everything

we've stolen or bought

(expensively) on it.

And it'll sit there sucking

water and when it burns up

we're fine to just grow another (sod).

Like history is so smoky and we

keep staring at the sun, going blind

until we're patriots too.

for Eileen

THE MINOR MIRACLES OF SAINT DIDACUS

Jasmine in each molecule we breathe

The fragrance of a wound held aloft

and measured potential to grow

Even in death to grow beside the body

corporeal or otherwise salt bearing

Penance and solitude call us too

from our lives as constant motion

or for lack of contemplating anything

really

before it is built or done

Like jasmine in the dreams of a healed king

Healing founder of measure and expense

ANOTHER MIRACLE OF SAINT DIDACUS

When the river held the valley together

without a bridge

As to look below and remember

nature was

more cynical about us

our buildings

full of people

and paperwork

and ennui

wobble a little

when earth shakes

without worship or ritual

When the river became a green trickle

Yellow and yellowing letters
asleep on paper for you

to awaken and employ
unfiltered in your daily.

The point is to say heart,
say breath, say now & there

its electricity scribbled
on what we touch like shivers.

There is nothing to be said
that can approximate solitude

not song, not dew, not boots
on the battlefield of innocence.

Trail of a finger on the window
in the shape of a heart

the sun comes through,
dust dances in it.

Nothing is done, the book isn't written,
isn't letterforms, ideas or intent.

We don't work like negative capability
does, everything in uncertainty.

I've got my ear to the glass.
I think you know how I feel.

Sand is always a median

on either side of which

everyone can be healed

by nearness to the body

Salt evaporates, makes the cool more temperate

without knowing a body

capable of perfume or piety

Sand washes down various rivers and

sand is pushed up from the seabed

These specks of stardust

on the edge of your bikini bottom

tiny golden worlds

cling to you

UNTITLED VISTA

I was looking for blue on a blown surface
the ocean's bifurcated horizon blue.

We advance on habitat with abandon.

I saw the business park impede the view
a wisp of cloud enough to say phantom dew.

Subtle chaparral where shipping centers are
I wanted a vision and got a wall.

Are we oscillations again, that sun machine?

To predict the survey (of land), I thought
she's kinda beautiful when the wind and sun do that.

Like to excavate the canyons I said parking lots
here, listen to their hollow thump.

We bang the drum of progress as if to row.

Blue leaves, blue paperwork, blue a window
to the brown day with clouds toned so sepia.

I've repeatedly wanted to leave, to drive home
and not have to drive back.

Starling that died on my hood, I'm still sorry.

PAPER NARCISSUS

Whose marble figure and laurelled crown could be electric, admired
enough to hum like the young poet or fall into an opening field.

October's endless ribbon in a maiden's hair I unravel, unknowing
of my disorder and ill reflection in this lily'd pool.

Whose wit and winsome idea to orbit, then make landfall like paper
birds do, like waterfall, like why are we all crying.

I'm lazy about writing these gossamer words, but what else is there
when October's burnt focus is on everything but me.

Whose deep noticing could force a paper-white narcissus in water
or make red paper more simple than reworking the legend.

The landscape of the human face—like my face in a mirror, returning to
places of childhood: home, destroyed home, a chimney, smoke.

Whose refugees congregate and are praying to whomever for what
they've lost: a little space, many tears, an ashen pool.

I think constantly about fashioning an ideal self that is this but with more
money and things and time to use these tools.

Rain is inside me and inside the soil, it is mud peeling off Rose Canyon
below a contentious idolater, and where the earth may split.

All of these things are happening now, like your heart is beating
inside you; and I, always traveling, wish it were inside me.

You are an arc of light in sycamore leaves,

churned-up dust, the sun's disturbance,

beside workers and workday traffic.

Bronze light in every space we inhabit.

This big sky we are under,

a portal without law.

Even poetry can't sample it.

It goes round rosy, always in motion,

like weather's coliseum lights.

+

One cloud changes the whole feel/field of things.
Afternoon indoor fluorescence, that silky envelope,
just a corner of blue window to see.

Pillars of smoke in our toxic and inefficient world,
smaller than it seems to be.

Outside, sounds approach like a shudder
without fantasy, a signal that we must go on
in fuzzy cubicles, a fraction of private space.

Light's decoy registers, safe in anybody's arms.

+

The brightness doesn't end here.

The filters don't stop it from coming through.

Particles invisible. Blue or gray day.

It is the way shrinking/rising things

can't be made dire enough.

I like your smile, I'd like to see it live on forever.

A line of cars and cars from here to vanishing-point's brown.

We cannot say sun, or sunlight, terminus,

stop where you see a sign.

SAINT DIDACUS IN THE LAND OF MIRACLES

A wave contains the exertion of many people

with a certain softness

a measure of mineral volume

the entire system of sand

At your doorstep and in the wind, a wave explains

nothing if it doesn't break and send flowers

of seawater, shell, and gold

We've built this city to honor energy, to use all

things sacred, even

water

isn't enough to base a hymn upon

So a wave at the steps contains many miracles

to heal a bankrupt pension

SET THE CONTROLS FOR THE HEART OF THE SUN

If we split the coast, would we be then bi-coastal
skipping stones through heron territory and rushes?

Being in a hurry always, trembling at dawn.

To bury the sound, the strings, to sing the shore's reach
to contact heat, we harmonies, the sound inside a shell.

The volume of words in speech.

If coast as long as poem, then success for the dead
for asphalt lanes, mile-marked with residue of carbon.

The ghosts are breaking the darkness.

If west is the way into the sun, everything I know is ash
you are ash, our voices are smoke and this is banned at the beach.

In unmoving cars, making the shape of a question.

If we run everything, all of this, aground or into the sun
your oil money and spurs won't pad your landing then.

THE BATONIST

If to get upsie-daisy is to right oneself
then I am not a flower wavering beneath the sun.

I forget about the poetry of morning, the birdies
in the fountain, the dew. . . I don't want to remember.

Not today, nor tomorrow. Is something twirling
up there in the sky, slender and chrome?

Each revolutionary gesture a sequined flair
of something meaningful, I guess. Something good.

Maybe it is just the effect of squinting through
the dirty windshield, past sleepy cars in rows.

Maybe gravity pulls on me a little more now
as if the last Newtonian fruit to fall from its tree.

Yet, I hold on to that ideal notion of artfully rising
spinning, always staying in motion. Even on the way down.

VERIFAX

We hear a lot of things: a warplane rehearsal

in blue or shuttle in, shuttle out like seeing

historicism lost in paradise.

We hear: I want to grow up to be . . . oh well.

You're just going to have to risk it.

We hear the most dangerous upbeat assessment,

a silver mushroom cloud

like violence rose and spread.

See the floating kaboom, a peaceful Buddha

smiling down on everyone.

I wanted paint instead of light

to pour from the mouth

into your open eyes, to let in

so much paint: thalo green,

a scratch of cadmium, celadon green.

At this time of day the sky

turns or is turning upon itself

like a storm in stop motion.

Decisions made will alter

everything

the future colors with regress.

There was this camera

that captured all human experimentation

and I wanted just a frame.

I wanted paint to rush up the sand

and over our feet, then dissolve.

The sun's penumbra in icky cinematic

light cast on our bad skin,

our bad dreams about good dreams.

PETROLATUM LENS TECHNIQUE

Like brightness saturates

the most impossible people,

like even every dull bulb in a vacuum

    like, yeah.

You know how blurry

these shapes are drawn

the yellow sun in the kiddie corner,

like a smudge.

To see, big eyes are the thing,

    even in fog

like the freeway slowed,

like syrup does.

To get lost in sad movie music,

it's impossible not to feel

fuzzy like brightness

just outside the theater.

The storyesque progression

is, like awesome

when it goes all multi-hued

and off kilter.

When brightness becomes your halo,

    it's just sun

and nothing holy.

It's the way the air around a palm

tree blurs

in the slightest bit of wind.

Like, beach weather

and all the people in worship

as the marine layer

puts its cold blanket to land.

TO MAKE YOU SURFER

In all the movies about California youth,
we are made to believe in gold everywhere.

In the sky, seaspray, and hair.

In neonesque cathedrals of sunlight, buildings in sand;
to think it must be easy to be an architect of simulacra.

In years I measure the length of your blonde
when subject to wind, its dusty sheen in the light.

In the motion of your hair, the sea in the sun,
a palm tree or row of palm trees done up with bows.

In a seascape town, inside a painting hums.

In all the movies we've said *killer, dude* and *no way*
it is these words that build in our mouths to establish place.

In evocation of torment, the sea is recurring.

In the rush of sound between us and the beach
the muscles struggle and move to make you surfer.

In the water, the words in your mouth widen with breath,
so to repeat them, weightless vapor evocatives.

In all the movies about California youth,
we are made, we are make believe.

DAYGLO

Now only banality still interests me.

—Chris Marker, from *Sans Soleil*

DAYGLO

Where the dark of rain and resilient sun
now meet, there glow the gears of day.
In gray, when the mind attributes color to an idea,
we offer a definite maybe for the sky's big cover-up.
If we are kept warm in sort-of-winter
it is the warmth of the sea-spray-blue sea.
The freeway's rush of hybrid cars and humming birds
should say something about nearness, and divergence,
but everything sloughs off.
Everything in the estuary, the alluvium
entering the ocean, a wet brown fan.
Great yellow dinosaurs of industry
remove any artifice from sculpture.
Mountains of earth rise from marshland
where we live background lives
with basketball hoops in the driveway.
A sporting chance for light to fill us.
Our digital children and their rapid-fire,
virtual dreams, I see them bug-eyed in backseats,
combat in every eye's reflection.
The glare and gauzy, anesthetic brightness
changes us, I know, my head a cloud
refracting what gray light passes through.

Behind every gesture lies a shadow,

an *idée fixe*.

The impedance of radiant light.

The dark below a sailor

different than the dark

below myself: Melville's etched sea.

How bars of light enter naptime,

horizontal and blinding, but we must push on.

There is the pattern of gulls to follow,

like the pattern on a scarf, on a woman's nape,

"I don't get *emotional densities*," in the museum,

or the cubes on the concourse floor.

With such roundness of light, and scope,

how can any line be so hard but the streak of train

as evening parades in exodus of squandered time.

So gradually progressing toward sea breeze, now

sandcastle, aubergine broadcast in the sky.

The way sun pushes into horizon

and we are warmed by it's flimsy bundle.

Look at the gaslamp now lit.

Look to the collapsing sky.

The shadows cast a cinematic shape

and so the people, redefined and shiny.

To not have an epiphany under partial sun

or fluorescence. No umbrella to manage the rain.

Not happiness in place of shimmer but happy

to have stepped on an oily puddle's rainbow.

To not have these things when clouded

and admire the floodplain, some water making way.

A paper boat with paraffin wax on its hull.

A few surfers get wet in the water,

black buoys on a silk gray sea.

There is less contrast in the world when rain.

The bombs we see as droplets are harmless.

The bombs we don't see are foreign and far off

as we try to keep dry.

Then the sun breaks through,

a little wink in the ether

so we wipe our dewy eyes, watch everything steam.

This is how mirage happens.

This is how to landscape with the Western Garden Book.

To not need water and know how to preserve it

within a well within oneself, to never be thirsty.

Say, go to the beach. Get some sun in your blonde

like these things we grow to let others tend.

To gather cancers on our skin, or soak

beneath a macular sky and brown,

we creep right up to the breakwater froth.

The glittery ceiling with sky's mirrorball.

Picture our time until now, beneath it,

is it possible to make a proof?

Beachums and bottle caps, a scrap of paper,

sand heaped up toward the tide-line,

dry kelp and a plastic thingy woven so in.

We use the palm tree defense,

just waver in the wind.

Never are we close enough to whisper.

We get breezy when the sea turns white

like the wet necessity for auto-immolation.

Then cancer more human than disease,

the human condition itself.

"Mommy, I want a soda."

I want the salt blue water of the sea

or that translucent haze in the eyes, tint

on the body's windows still golden all over.

Seashell, a bright towel on the sand is all.

I see people in shorts in too early Spring.

Morning's cinema curtain pulled back.

Living things chirp in the shrubs,

traffic's quiet silver drone behind them.

I can barely see you through the fog,

or you are not even there, just dew's morphology.

How we are like the sky—dust and light:

blue—a reflection of what floats around us.

Did you know that even the air is an ocean?

We swim in it while staring at the water, thinking.

To think I know you,

I have read your chapter book.

Your brick and mortar composition,

graffiti on the wall: *ORPHAN, THUGZ,*

I Heart Jenny, gun and a funny-face, now vacant.

Even the jacaranda's purple laugh

isn't a frail or lonely translation.

The radio news with its public hem,

while I drive around the block.

I drive around the block again.

I drive around the block looking to park and see anything

for more than a flash and you drive too.

The timbre of city noise beneath the overpass.

The whiteness of its echo between studious pillars,

rumble of languor and amenity.

Hear a zephyr inside the soft racket,

it moves you just so.

A palm frond and grocery bag in mid-air,

moving too. Say, "I am not here.

I am nowhere listening to nothing."

A mere adjunct of someplace glamorous,

some burning satellite of a bigger world.

This is where I stepped down from the upper crust,

needless science in place of silence.

But it is not so much the noise,

it is the quiet coo,

ambivalent and pedestrian with sunshiny hue.

Even the sun does a soundscape thing.

A far-off fanfare of timbrel shimmers,

cricket whir between the rushes and horizon.

Brakes and brakes and brakes.

You could say this is an affect of the sun

with no thisness at all, just a nest of bi-ways,

some birds there, making a racket.

We are all shiny surfaces, windows and silk,

streets cleaned with water

to take on the stain of morning sun.

A bird's broadcast song broken by the cough

of the combustion engine.

I become the glare of earthly sounds,

the culture of noise, I am only a participant.

I adore you. "Whatever's ok."

Some small account reflected in every face,

like the history of palm trees (money)

and fake boobs (debt).

Do we ever put down roots?

Put our city where our mouths are,

watch all the cars pour out of it.

Pull the yellow tickets from our wiper blades.

Tickets paid for with strawberries.

A wad of newsprint says, "Illegal immigrants,

a variable in the horizon."

Not the sun's horizon, but the future,

now in flux or folly, though we want it clear.

I saw a soldier today.

We aren't just built on soldiering, a mighty field,

ACU-digital camouflage on our skateboards.

Put your cool logo wherever.

Against the canvas of sky the hills are fire.

We are accustomed to this

in summer. In our land of sun and fire.

The sea are burning too. Not rain or wind.

Dumb human animal with cigarette (likely).

Dumb American.

East of the sea where night glows

instead of that slit of light entering the water

coming and going water.

On a map of the West

the westernmost edge

more shallow with each revision.

Like youth and reading, somnambulism and art.

The fire, a shallow vision, tumescent

but only in flame. To just put it out.

Boots, nozzle, spray, steam.

We fire-engines of hope.

Red to the mind like apple catches.

No rain but lightning and dry brush.

O summer without apology,

I have lost my heart for too much thisness.

Too many *ding-dongs* and too many fires left on.

So to what do we look?

The canvas of sky, a dumb American, a silhouette.

Thunderheads parenting the eastern sky

puffy clouds too can be Zeus-like

and strike down their own children

in whatever forms they take:

pampas grass, oak tree, dusty stream bed.

A presidential anvil

presides over summer's blunt object

—I'm saying there are big, big clouds—

but nature is absent from talk radio.

The discussion is devolutionary at best

when god comes in and common sense goes out.

Things evolve like love does,

like systems that are in place to keep us turning,

keep us safe, or in a bit of progress.

The airwaves wield a bolt of lightning.

The chatter is always listened to without privacy.

Sometimes the thunder is only a broken sound barrier,

practice for war,

the nature of war in sagebrush alongside the airfield.

FA-18 Hornets boom above the freeway

as eucalyptus leaves rustle.

This is the way home, this every day.

In an outpost of an olde republic mind,

I listen to the room and its silences.

I am becoming a silent container.

The burst of wind, warm and up

from the desert, moves eucalypts to break

and scatter their foreign parts like genealogy does.

If I had nothing to do with this sprawl

I would not live in it like a particle of dust.

I don't know why living is a problematic thing.

The sun is always just the sun.

Its moving picture a projection imagined

like silent cinema, like everyone

huddled on beach blankets watching

the doomsday clock.

But the big end will be a big surprise,

we'll all be desert again, be dust.

How the transaction between people

and place happens

when it becomes part of what we do.

Like my affinity for here is always moving

away, then returning home. That's the idea:

change something and pretend it's new.

INTERTIDAL TISSUE

Connective tissue in concrete

mapping a kind of alien topography

To look down through the gold

like to determine the clarity of diamonds (sky)

Smoke and fog as emissions go

a lovely Rubine© sunset print

I told you to quit miming

the existential behavior of office work

Traffic is a fact of life

So are allergens

Things that move through the air

Red Knot, Brown Pelican, Cinnamon Teal

Anna's Hummingbird

We maintain that movement is a private thing

FINEST CITY

FINEST CITY

There are pieces of you in the harbor,

pieces of you in the foam.

If to collect them and say   "this is how to protect a vessel."

The gibbous reflection of a keel,

of industry's habitual maritime in the bay.

Up on the flight deck of America's pleasure-boat

someone lost a feather in the wind like cannon fodder.

The sailors dressed in whites

spelling out VICTORY!

Says the shroud, a corset of war: "I wane for you when I'm going home."

To read the way in Spanish cartography,

how shadow and light pull

out of the harbor, up onto the esplanade.

A child to his father,   "whose salt water in my taffy?"

An island made to embrace the big dream:

galleons to fund our city summary

in wartime, again in wartime now.

Its constant stutter of aircraft sound,

the white noise we live with.

Helicopter the coastline, a freed balloon.

Apache, Sea Knight, Super Stallion

hover and rattle the tables,

cut the air and the sun we are taxed for.

So to want without war in the sun,

to be at war with what we question.

PET SOUNDS, OR A BETTER CHANCE TO STUDY PRACTICAL CETOLOGY

It is the whiteness of the whale, the blackness

of the whale that below fireworks

each evening, must become a colored

and toothsome smile. The whale

in captivity on the bay sings

to his audience like his mother sang

to me as a child.

It is a manifestation of culture,

this connection between singer and who sung to.

    My wettest neighbor,

I know thy dialect whose clicks and whistles

rile children to their feet.

The open blue sky today, like the small blue pool

without enclosure. Do you perform to be free?

    Do you believe?

It is not an idle whim that you salute

with a spyhop or a splash, it is your mechanism

that makes you, by definition, a nationless patriot.

But here we are to be toneblind, the theory

of color, a tercet: red, white, blue.

How you are painted so, no Tyndall effect

be done, but with inverse agitprop and corporation.

Our soapbox theatre, O do you hear?

The ear of the whale, what does

it translate from the cheers and spectacle.

Every day the jets ascend,

their rhythm like waves booming upon the valley.

The noise we don't hear but feel a part of,

a constant wall around us,

and birdsong from a cage next door.

To be captive,

to make song of captivity, to smile

or appear to smile because that is your face.

The whiteness and the blackness of your face you smile.

A stable of whales—*Orcinus Orca*—

we know your stage name: not blackfish

nor seawolf, gentle hunter of the seas.

The head not a Roman chariot

lashed aside the Pequod, but skyward torpedo

of opposite values.

Do you speak to one another of openness

of instinct, or is it so removéd, so

please and so thank you.

Wouldn't it be nice

if the glassine replica were on sale?
If teleology were universal as I settle down
and into my work with words to equate ideas
of freedom and captivity. Am I where
I should be? Is the ocean in your bones?
The souvenir form a trapped echo, or
resonant slogan so purely American
as a foamy head. To be drunk on patriotism
in a tank. In the bleachers around the tank.

      I salute you.

AN HISTORIE, AN INVERSE STRUCTURE

At once an utterance and then a song for

direction established like a compass magnet

to history's repetitive North.

I see you and can say there is room at the table

    for all of us.

There are pathways and bomb-shelters

still, and we are learning in the eucalyptus grove

there is a metal tree so like a radio.

We are wont to steal the linguistics of

—without leaves and without remorse—

its emanating voice.

+

What library isn't full of periodical sadness?

    All of the dead.

What is noble in being taught, is noble in being said,

so to become an echo,

a living and youthful inheritor of someone

    whom I've read.

Neither fables of poetry or objects of wood

are alive, but they are certain and real.

Under an invisible, birdless sky,

the actual beach receives them

here in its various jars.

+

To write the vibrations of a place and

hear sun coming through the neighborhood

or assign a letter to a shadow

—purple mountains' majesty—

everything is nothing's consolation.

A charge of spindrift between them.

A coastline flecked with starlite

                gives us nothing.

Stars dropping down from space into all of us

to turn the lights on.

It is enough to feel that relief

of having a bed to read, then sleep, upon.

ROCK TO FAKIE

Whose emotion in an empty pool,

performing on wheels a composition,

a 50/50 grind and kick flip there,

a picture of youth's trajectory.

Because words evolve in sport and speaking,

even everything said barely means a nickel to me.

I imagine the thrill of falling and not falling

(sticking it) just ordinary.

There are too many eyes watching

each genuflection's technique.

Here a ramp, there a rail.

They call that form "the volcano"

and I guess it does rise from a bowl.

Bodies erupt from it, a *lien air* to a safe transition.

I watch your body blur in the distance,

on a learning curve,

the whole visible world held still.

for Brighton

IN ORBIT

The waves innumerably come and fade
like age begets deliberation

There never was a here to be had
but loss of space and keeled mind

Triumphal blackness

Is a speck of light I didn't see
available to the eye's inversion

A macrocosm of minimalism

The waves are in my body's instruments
as breath's machination

To go and be gone, to inhale
without commune, to breathe

To be free, to free

IF TO WHISPER, THEN

It is gold here
in silence, how

a mourning dove
observes daybreak

or a breeze rustles
nothing so

we hear what imagines
us in colored regalia

Now gold here
in silence, no

whisper or trumpets
to declare

we have lived
a good American life

surrounded by everyone

we've ever loved.

for Mary Alice Johnson (1911-2008)

In this canyon of honey business

where other Indian name

is an unexplained

    place-name

so pleasant a nickname

the spiritualist Harmony,

from the end of the Civil War

and petroglyphs

I can still read through the wear

    place-named

for rainmaking fame

and a folk-fossil of frustration

He came West, settled

at the mouth of a canyon

after the Civil War

honey flowed from it

From the Spanish for isolation,

woman of isolation.

There is a wind

in the mouth of translation

in the translated words for

solitude and solace,

where the stone cross

makes a sun-dial.

Is a body discovered

or place-name

of the Christianized tribe's rancheria

bestowed on the hilltop?

It is what we fight over now

and fought in Spanish Colonial times.

TO BUILD A LAGOON (WHERE AN ESTUARY IS)

Scrape again the soil away and scrape a nesting
a habitat in foggy spring morning.

Indicate absolute ecology to be traveled through
in foggy morning commuter lanes.

How brilliantine the sunrise in shallow pools
the estuary filled with runoff and diversion.

Bring birds and nesting birds to be viewed
the daily scraping for ugliness to remind us.

Construct a salt marsh for the current's reversal
berms and the Pacific Flyway's landing strip.

Labor to simulate original soil, grasses, and tufts
or define nature as it disappears.

Know beauty exists only in contrast
or is paid for by all we can ever expect.

EUCALYPTOID

Leafy pendulum in a color-field, say

floating leaf, dancing light, an emblem

for depth evolving into question,

a question of space.

The way we inhabit space,

air in the space that carries us,

and us, our alveoli,

the quality of air within our lungs.

I speak in thoughts formed with air.

Where fog makes a window frown,

a little white sound to fill the gray area,

the tug and tumble of people speaking

like we are the natural world's syncopation.

Diesel apparitions like branches

in the light of day's whoosh

and white commotion, an utterance.

Who is anyone to say?

What is our endeavor?

The din continues until there is emptiness.

This or that breath, unlike registers of wind,

unlike the dissonant road, or flight, or sun

coming down on every machine

and living thing with equal force.

A tree doesn't ask about its purpose.

NOTES

Saint Didacus (c. 1400-1463) is the saint for whom San Diego was named.

"Set the Controls for the Heart of the Sun" takes its name from the song on Pink Floyd's second record, *A Saucerful of Secrets*. It is the only recording to feature both Syd Barrett and David Gilmour.

"I Saw the Bolex of My Dreams" is a quote taken from an interview with David Lynch, and refers to his early short film *Six Men Getting Sick*.

"Pet Sounds, or A Better Chance to Study Practical Cetology" samples the ground-breaking Beach Boys record and Herman Melville's cetological observations in *Moby Dick*.

"John Harbison, Pioneer and Innovative Bee Keeper" and "Village of Our Lady Solitude" are altered erasures of passages in Lou Stein's *San Diego County Place-Names* and reference Harbison Canyon and Soledad Mountain, respectively.

———

ABOUT THE AUTHOR

JAMES MEETZE is the author of *I Have Designed This For You* (2007), and editor, with Simon Pettet, of *Other Flowers: Uncollected Poems by James Schuyler* (2010).

Ahsahta Press

Ahsahta Press

NEW SERIES

This book is set in Apollo MT type with Century Gothic titles
by Ahsahta Press at Boise State University
and printed by Thomson-Shore, Inc.
Cover design by Quemadura.
Book design by Janet Holmes.

AHSAHTA PRESS

2011

JANET HOLMES, DIRECTOR
JODI CHILSON, MANAGING EDITOR

KAT COE	GENNA KOHLHARDT
CHRIS CRAWFORD	BREONNA KRAFFT
TIMOTHY DAVIS	MATT TRUSLOW
CHARLES GABEL	ZACH VESPER
KATE HOLLAND	EVAN WESTERFIELD